Cambridge
Key English Test
3

Examination papers from University of Cambridge ESOL Examinations: English for Speakers of Other Languages

CAMBRIDGE
UNIVERSITY PRESS

PUBLISHED BY THE PRESS SYNDICATE OF THE UNIVERSITY OF CAMBRIDGE
The Pitt Building, Trumpington Street, Cambridge, United Kingdom

CAMBRIDGE UNIVERSITY PRESS
The Edinburgh Building, Cambridge CB2 2RU, UK
40 West 20th Street, New York NY 10011–4211, USA
477 Williamstown Road, Port Melbourne, VIC 3207, Australia
Ruiz de Alarcón 13, 28014 Madrid, Spain
Dock House, The Waterfront, Cape Town 8001, South Africa

http://www.cambridge.org

© Cambridge University Press 2003

This book is in copyright, which normally means that no reproduction of any part may take place without the written permission of Cambridge University Press. The copying of certain parts of it by individuals for use within the classroom, however, is permitted without such formality. Pages which are copiable without further permission are identified by a separate copyright notice:
© UCLES K&J Photocopiable

First published 2003
Reprinted 2003

Printed in the United Kingdom at the University Press, Cambridge

Typeface Helvetica 10/13pt. *System* QuarkXPress® [OD&I]

A catalogue record for this book is available from the British Library

ISBN 0 521 75478 X Student's Book
ISBN 0 521 75479 8 Student's Book with Answers
ISBN 0 521 75480 1 Teacher's Book
ISBN 0 521 75482 8 Audio CD
ISBN 0 521 75481 X Cassette

Contents

Acknowledgements 4

To the student 5

Test 1   Paper 1   6
             Paper 2   18
             Paper 3   25

Test 2   Paper 1   26
             Paper 2   38
             Paper 3   45

Test 3   Paper 1   46
             Paper 2   58
             Paper 3   65

Test 4   Paper 1   66
             Paper 2   78
             Paper 3   85

Visual materials for Paper 3 86

Sample answer sheets 94

Acknowledgements

The publishers are grateful for permission to reproduce copyright material. It has not always been possible to identify the sources of all the material used, and in such cases the publishers would welcome information from the copyright owners.

Illustrations by David Eaton

Book design by Peter Ducker MSTD

Cover design by Dunne & Scully

The cassette/CD which accompanies this book was recorded at Studio AVP, London.

To the student

This book is for students preparing for the University of Cambridge ESOL Examinations Key English Test (KET). It contains four complete tests based on the new test format from March 2004.

What is KET?

KET is an examination for students of English as a foreign language. It tests Reading, Writing, Listening and Speaking. The KET examination is at Cambridge Level One (Council of Europe Level A2).

Paper 1	1 hour 10 minutes	**Reading and Writing**	9 parts	50% of total marks
Paper 2	about 30 minutes	**Listening**	5 parts	25% of total marks
Paper 3	8–10 minutes	**Speaking**	2 parts	25% of total marks

How do I prepare for KET?

It is important to know what type of questions are in the KET examination. Doing the tests in this book will help you. Practise putting your answers on the sample answer sheets on pages 94–96 (you may photocopy these pages). This will help you to understand what you have to do in the real test.

Reading: Read some books in simple English from your library or local bookshop. Try to guess the words you don't know before you use a dictionary to check them. Also, use an English learner's dictionary when you study. If you live in a tourist area, there may be some signs or notices in English outside restaurants and shops or in railway stations and airports. Read these and try to understand them.

Writing: Write short letters or messages in English to a friend who is learning English with you or find an English-speaking pen-friend to write to. Write about your daily life (your home, work or school and your family). If you go on holiday, write postcards in English and send them to your English-speaking friends.

Listening: Listen to the cassettes that come with English course books so you can hear different people speaking English. Watch English-language programmes on television and listen to English on the radio if possible.

Speaking: Talk in English with friends who are studying with you. Ask each other questions about your daily lives, your future plans and about other towns, countries or places you have visited.

We hope this book helps you when you take the KET examination. Good luck!

Test 1

PAPER 1   READING AND WRITING (1 hour 10 minutes)

PART 1
QUESTIONS 1–5

Which notice (A–H) says this (1–5)?
For questions 1–5, mark the correct letter A–H on the answer sheet.

EXAMPLE	ANSWER
0 We work fast.	H

1   This is not for adults.

2   You can't drive this way.

3   We can help you day and night.

4   You can have dinner here.

5   Come here to book a holiday.

A   YOUTH CLUB
Under 16s only

B   *Half-price drinks with 3-course meals!*

C   CITY CENTRE CLOSED TO TRAFFIC ALL DAY TODAY

D   *Tourist Information open 24 hours*

E   NO PETROL STATION ON MOTORWAY

F   TURNER TRAVEL
Fly away to the sun this summer

G   SCHOOL OFFICE CLOSED FOR LUNCH

H   We repair shoes **QUICKLY**
8 a.m. – 5 p.m.

Paper 1   Reading and Writing

PART 2

QUESTIONS 6–10

Read the sentences (6–10) about Sam's new computer.
Choose the best word (A, B or C) for each space.
For questions 6–10, mark A, B or C on the answer sheet.

EXAMPLE	ANSWER
0 Sam's father .... him a new computer for his birthday.	A
A bought **B** paid **C** spent	

---

6   He .... Sam how to use it.

   A learnt   **B** showed   **C** studied

7   Sam sent an e-mail .... to his friend Billy to tell him about his nice present.

   A message   **B** programme   **C** form

8   Billy came to Sam's house and they did their geography .... together.

   A subject   **B** homework   **C** class

9   They were .... because they found some information about rivers on the internet.

   A happy   **B** interesting   **C** pleasant

10   Afterwards, they .... playing a new computer game together.

   A wanted   **B** thanked   **C** enjoyed

Test 1

PART 3

QUESTIONS 11–15

Complete the five conversations.
For questions 11–15, mark A, B or C on the answer sheet.

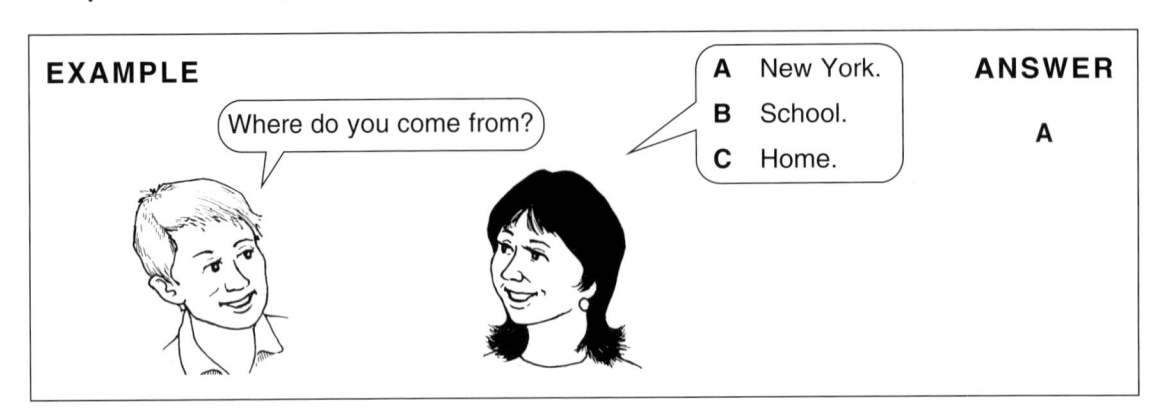

EXAMPLE

Where do you come from?

A   New York.
B   School.
C   Home.

ANSWER

A

---

11   Who's that man with the green sweater?

A   He's my brother.
B   It's John's.
C   I don't know it.

12   Where's Amanda gone?

A   She's at the station.
B   She'll arrive tomorrow.
C   She's going to leave tonight.

13   I hate shopping.

A   So do I.
B   Certainly.
C   That's all right.

14   How long did the journey take?

A   About 500 kilometres.
B   Almost 5 hours.
C   Last week.

15   The room costs £55 a night.

A   I don't take it.
B   Give me two, please.
C   That's a lot.

Paper 1   Reading and Writing

QUESTIONS 16–20

Complete the conversation in a garage.
What does David say to the mechanic?
For questions 16–20, mark the correct letter A–H on the answer sheet.

EXAMPLE		ANSWER
Mechanic:	Good morning. How can I help you?	
David:	0	E

Mechanic: Certainly. What's the problem?

David: **16** ....

Mechanic: How long have you had the car?

David: **17** ....

Mechanic: Hm, there may be something wrong with the engine.

David: **18** ....

Mechanic: I'm afraid we have a lot of work at the moment. I can't do it until Friday.

David: **19** ....

Mechanic: Well, I suppose I can do it on Wednesday.

David: **20** ....

Mechanic: Bring it in at 8.30 in the morning.

A   Oh dear. Can you repair it now?

B   That will be fine.

C   Thanks. How much will it cost?

D   It's only Monday today. I'll go to another garage.

E   Would you have a look at my car, please?

F   I bought it new about four years ago.

G   It goes at eighty kilometres an hour.

H   It won't start in the morning.

9

PART 4

QUESTIONS 21–27

Read the article about Howard Bonnier.
Are sentences 21–27 'Right' (A) or 'Wrong' (B)?
If there is not enough information to answer 'Right' (A) or 'Wrong' (B), choose 'Doesn't say' (C).
For questions 21–27, mark A, B or C on the answer sheet.

HOWARD BONNIER

Bray is a beautiful village about fifty kilometres west of London. A young Englishman named Howard Bonnier opened a restaurant called *The Palace* there about three and a half months ago. Not many people in Britain know Mr Bonnier's name yet, but he's already quite famous in France. This is because he has written in French magazines about almost all the best restaurants in that country. He's only 29 years old.

When Howard was a teenager, he often went to restaurants with his mother and father. He liked doing this so much that he decided not to buy lots of clothes and CDs; instead, he used his money to visit France and eat in good restaurants. He also bought a lot of French and English cookbooks – he says he has more than two hundred and fifty!

So why did he decide to open a restaurant? Simply because he loves cooking. Has it been an easy thing to do? He says it's expensive to start your own restaurant and it's much more difficult to cook for fifty people than to cook for your family, but he's sure he's done the right thing.

Paper 1   Reading and Writing

EXAMPLE	ANSWER
0 Howard is French.	**B**
A Right **B** Wrong **C** Doesn't say	

21   *The Palace* has been open for less than a year.

A   Right   **B**   Wrong   **C**   Doesn't say

22   Lots of people in France know about Howard.

A   Right   **B**   Wrong   **C**   Doesn't say

23   Howard's parents took him out to restaurants.

A   Right   **B**   Wrong   **C**   Doesn't say

24   Howard has always spent a lot of money on clothes.

A   Right   **B**   Wrong   **C**   Doesn't say

25   Howard has written books about French cooking.

A   Right   **B**   Wrong   **C**   Doesn't say

26   It costs a lot of money to eat in Howard's restaurant.

A   Right   **B**   Wrong   **C**   Doesn't say

27   Howard says cooking for a lot of people is easy.

A   Right   **B**   Wrong   **C**   Doesn't say

PART 5

QUESTIONS 28–35

Read the article about line dancing.
Choose the best word (A, B or C) for each space (28–35).
For questions 28–35, mark A, B or C on the answer sheet.

Line dancing

Thousands of people in Britain ......**0**...... a new hobby – line dancing. In almost ......**28**...... town, you will find clubs and classes for this new activity.

'Line dancing is easy to learn. If you have two feet and can walk, then you can do it!' Fiona Lever, a teacher, ...**29**...... . 'You don't need a partner because you dance ......**30**...... groups. It's the ......**31**...... way to make new friends. In my classes, ...**32**...... are young and old people. The boys like it because they can make a lot of noise with their feet ......**33**...... the dances!'

When ......**34**...... line dancing begin? Most people think it started about fifteen years ......**35**...... when American country music became famous in Britain.

	EXAMPLE					ANSWER
0	A have	B	had	C	having	A

28	A	all	B	some	C	every
29	A	say	B	says	C	saying
30	A	at	B	to	C	in
31	A	best	B	better	C	good
32	A	here	B	there	C	they
33	A	among	B	across	C	during
34	A	has	B	is	C	did
35	A	after	B	ago	C	since

Test 1

PART 6

QUESTIONS 36–40

Read the descriptions (36–40) of some things you may find in your bag.
What is the word for each description?
The first letter is already there. There is one space for each other letter in the word.
For questions 36–40, write the words on the answer sheet.

EXAMPLE	ANSWER
0 You use this to write with.	p _e_ _n_

36 If you lose this, you won't be able to get into your house.   k _ _

37 Many people put these on when they want to read something.   g _ _ _ _ _ _

38 People pay for things with this.   m _ _ _ _

39 If it has been windy, you may need to do your hair with this.   c _ _ _

40 You write important dates in this so you don't forget them.   d _ _ _ _

PART 7

QUESTIONS 41–50

Complete this letter.
Write ONE word for each space (41–50).
For questions 41–50, write your words on the answer sheet.

Dear Lynne and Tony,

I'm writing (**Example:** ...to...) say thank you ...**41**... the two nights I stayed in ...**42**... lovely home. It ...**43**... good to see you again.

Here ...**44**... the photographs ...**45**... your children that you asked for. They're good photos, aren't ...**46**... ? I hope you like ...**47**... . I really love my new camera.

I ...**48**... going to visit my sister in New York next week. I ...**49**... take a lot of photos there, too. I haven't seen my sister for a long ...**50**... .

Thanks again.

Love,

Roy

Test 1

PART 8

QUESTIONS 51–55

Read the two e-mail messages.
Fill in the information on the visa application form.
For questions 51–55, write the information on the answer sheet.

To:	Churchill Language School, Oxford
From:	Alice Silveiro

I would like to study at your school. I work in the reception of a hotel in my home town, Sao Paulo, Brazil, and English is important for my job.

Where can I stay in Oxford? I shall spend two months in Britain.

Alice Silveiro

To:	Alice Silveiro
From:	Churchill Language School, Oxford

We have six-week courses for people who want to study English. There is a house for students next to the school, in Park Road, at number 26.

You will need a visa.

Churchill Language School

VISA APPLICATION FORM

Name: *Alice Silveiro*

Nationality: **51**

Job: **52**

Address in Britain: **53**

Why are you visiting Britain? **54**

How long will you stay? **55**

Paper 1 Reading and Writing

PART 9

QUESTION 56

Read this postcard from your friend, Paul.

POSTCARD

I'm very pleased you're going to visit me on Saturday. How will you get here? What time will you arrive? What shall we do?

See you soon.

Yours,

        Paul

Write Paul a postcard. Answer his questions.
Write 25–35 words.
Write your postcard on the answer sheet.

17

PAPER 2 LISTENING (approximately 30 minutes including 8 minutes transfer time)

PART 1

QUESTIONS 1–5

You will hear five short conversations.
You will hear each conversation twice.
There is one question for each conversation.
For questions 1–5, put a tick ✓ under the right answer.

EXAMPLE

0 How many people were at the meeting?

3	13	30
A ☐	B ☐	C ✓

---

1 When did Gary start his new job?

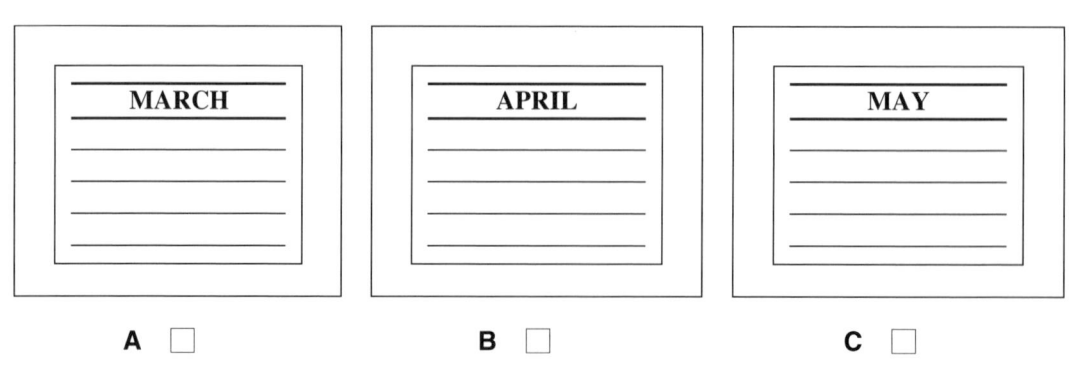

MARCH	APRIL	MAY
A ☐	B ☐	C ☐

2 What time does the film start?

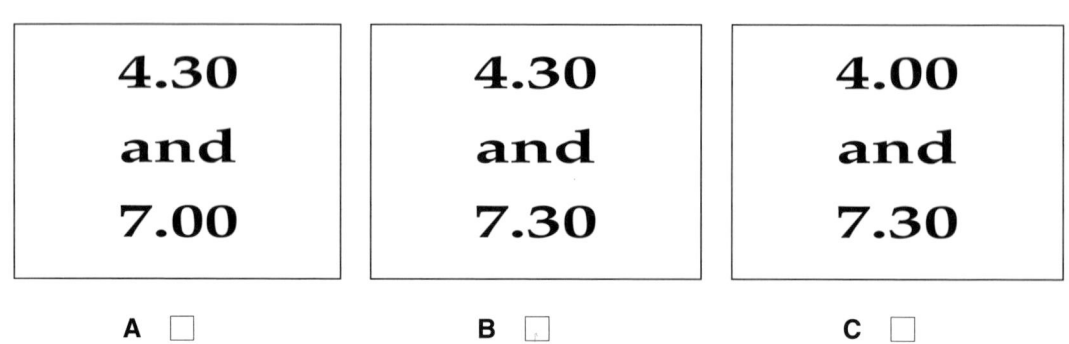

4.30 and 7.00	4.30 and 7.30	4.00 and 7.30
A ☐	B ☐	C ☐

Paper 2   Listening

3   What was the weather like on Saturday?

A ☐   B ☐   C ☐

4   Which motorway will they take?

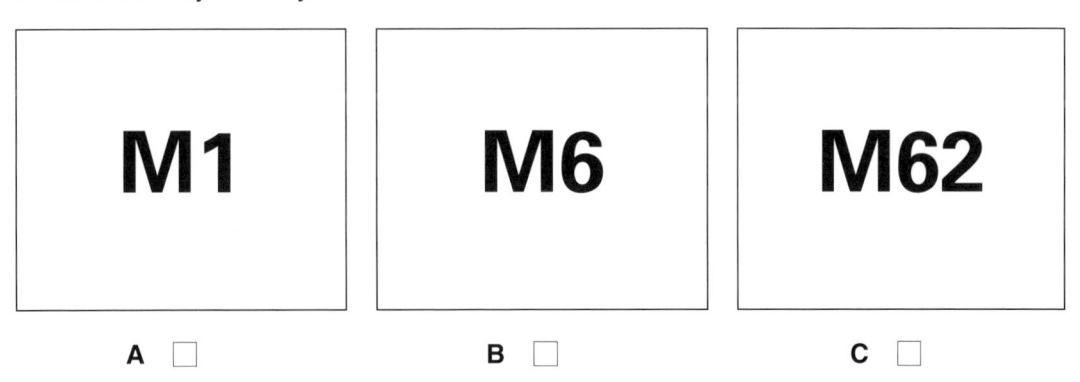

M1   M6   M62

A ☐   B ☐   C ☐

5   Which book does Lorna want?

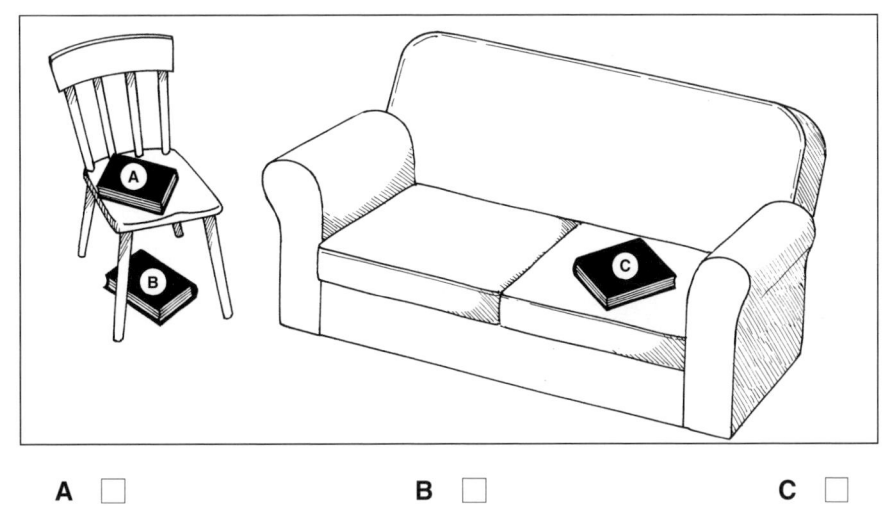

A ☐   B ☐   C ☐

Test 1

PART 2

QUESTIONS 6–10

Listen to Sue talking to a friend about her new clothes.
Why did Sue decide to buy each thing?
For questions 6–10, write a letter A–H next to the clothes.
You will hear the conversation twice.

EXAMPLE

0   jeans   F

CLOTHES SUE BOUGHT   **WHY?**

6   jacket   ☐   A   big

                               B   cheap

7   dress   ☐
                               C   expensive

8   sweater ☐
                               D   light

                               E   long

9   coat   ☐

                               F   purple

10 t-shirt ☐
                               G   short

                               H   soft

20

Paper 2   Listening

PART 3

QUESTIONS 11–15

Listen to Jan talking to Steve about getting a student travel card.
For questions 11–15, tick ✓ A, B or C.
You will hear the conversation twice.

EXAMPLE		ANSWER
0 How is Steve going to go to London?		
A	by bus	☐
B	by car	☐
C	by train	✓

11 How much is a travel card?

    A   £6 ☐

    B   £16 ☐

    C   £60 ☐

12 Jan will need

    A   one photo. ☐

    B   two photos. ☐

    C   four photos. ☐

13 Photos are less expensive

    A   in the photographer's shop. ☐

    B   in the library. ☐

    C   in the post office. ☐

Test 1

14 For the travel card, Jan must take

    A a letter.

    B her passport.

    C her driving licence.

15 Jan can get a travel card from

    A her college.

    B the travel agent's.

    C the tourist office.

PART 4

QUESTIONS 16–20

You will hear a man speaking on the telephone.
Listen and complete questions 16–20.
You will hear the conversation twice.

TELEPHONE MESSAGE

To:		Mr Brown
From:	**16**	David
Not in school because he has:	**17**	a bad
Students should read pages:	**18**	.... to ....
David will return to school on:	**19**	.... afternoon
at:	**20**	.... p.m.

Test 1

PART 5

QUESTIONS 21–25

You will hear some information about a pop concert.
Listen and complete questions 21–25.
You will hear the information twice.

POP CONCERT

Name of group: Red River

In London: From: October 28th

To: **21** November ....

Price of ticket: **22** £ ....

Telephone no: **23** ....

Place: **24** .... Bank Hall

In: **25** .... Street

You now have 8 minutes to write your answers on the answer sheet.

PAPER 3   SPEAKING (8–10 minutes)

The Speaking test lasts 8 to 10 minutes. You will take the test with another candidate. There are two examiners, but only one of them will talk to you. The examiner will ask you questions and ask you to talk to the other candidate.

Part 1 (5–6 minutes)

The examiner will ask you and your partner some questions. These questions will be about your daily life, past experience and future plans. For example, you may have to speak about your school, job, hobbies or home town.

Part 2 (3–4 minutes)

You and your partner will speak to each other. You will ask and answer questions. The examiner will give you a card with some information on it. The examiner will give your partner a card with some words on it. Your partner will use the words on the card to ask you questions about the information you have. Then you will change roles.

Test 2

PAPER 1   READING AND WRITING (1 hour 10 minutes)

PART 1
QUESTIONS 1–5

Which notice (A–H) says this (1–5)?
For questions 1–5, mark the correct letter A–H on the answer sheet.

EXAMPLE	ANSWER
0 You can't come in here.	D

1   You can't leave your bicycle here.

2   Adults shouldn't let children play with this.

3   You can buy children's clothes here.

4   Do not come in if you are not wearing the right clothes.

5   Use this door to go outside.

A   School Uniform Department – This floor

B   DANGER! No hard hat? No boots? NO ENTRANCE

C   NO BICYCLES AGAINST THIS WINDOW

D   KEEP OUT

E   BICYCLES ONLY

F   Exit to Shoemaker Road

G   DANGER! KEEP AWAY FROM CHILDREN

H   BICYCLES TO RENT
    Adults   £3.50 per hour
    Children   £2.00 per hour

Paper 1   Reading and Writing

PART 2

QUESTIONS 6–10

Read the sentences (6–10) about going to a new school.
Choose the best word (A, B or C) for each space.
For questions 6–10, mark A, B or C on the answer sheet.

EXAMPLE			ANSWER
0 It was the morning of Sally's first .... at her new school.			B
A moment	B day	C hour	

6   Sally felt rather .... because she didn't know anybody.

   A   unhappy   B   poor   C   single

7   The teacher .... Sally to the classroom.

   A   put   B   went   C   took

8   Sally sat next to a girl with blonde .... called Amy.

   A   eyes   B   teeth   C   hair

9   At lunchtime, Amy gave Sally an apple and .... her all about the school.

   A   told   B   learned   C   spoke

10 By the end of the afternoon, Amy was Sally's .... friend.

   A   lovely   B   best   C   excellent

27

Test 2

PART 3

QUESTIONS 11–15

Complete the five conversations.
For conversations 11–15, mark A, B or C on the answer sheet.

EXAMPLE

How are you?

A I'm 18.
B I'm Sally.
C I'm fine.

ANSWER

C

11   £500 is too expensive.

A Not many.
B Why not?
C I agree.

12   I've got an appointment with my doctor today.

A How does he feel?
B What's the matter with you?
C Who do you want?

13   Would you like anything else?

A That's all, thank you.
B Yes, I like everything.
C Two, please.

14   When is your mother's birthday?

A She's thirty-nine.
B It was last week.
C It's a long time.

15   Shall we go to the shops now?

A I'm too tired.
B They're very good.
C Not at all.

QUESTIONS 16–20

Complete the conversation at an airport.
What does Stephen say to the airport assistant?
For questions 16–20, mark the correct letter A–H on the answer sheet.

EXAMPLE		ANSWER
Assistant:	Good morning. Can I see your ticket, please?	
Stephen:	0	G

Assistant:	You're going to fly to Scotland?	A	Well, I suppose I can get something to eat. Where's the restaurant?
Stephen:	16		
Assistant:	I'm sorry, but there's a short delay because of fog.	B	Here's my passport.
Stephen:	17	C	Yes, that's right. I'm going to visit my family.
Assistant:	About an hour. It won't be any more.		
Stephen:	18	D	By the window, please.
Assistant:	It's on the first floor. Can I take your suitcases now, please?	E	Yes, but not this bag. Is it all right to take it on the plane?
Stephen:	19	F	That's bad news. How long for?
Assistant:	Yes, you can take one piece of luggage with you. Where would you like to sit?	G	Yes, here you are.
Stephen:	20	H	Can I smoke if I sit there?
Assistant:	There you are. Number 24A. Enjoy your trip.		

PART 4

QUESTIONS 21–27

Read the article about a writer.

Are sentences 21–27 'Right' (A) or 'Wrong' (B)?

If there is not enough information to answer 'Right' (A) or 'Wrong' (B), choose 'Doesn't say' (C).

For questions 21–27, mark A, B or C on the answer sheet.

Bill Prince-Smith

Bill Prince-Smith was a farmer and a teacher and a dentist before he became a writer of children's books at the age of 60. Now, thirteen years later, he has written more than 80 books. Every day, he goes into his office and writes. In the evening, he gives the work to his wife to read. 'She tells me when she doesn't like something,' says Bill. 'My ten grandchildren don't live near here but they also read my stories and say if they are good or bad.' And so Bill has learned what young children want to read.

Bill writes about the life in his village and on the farms near it. His fifth book is his favourite: *The Sheepdog* is about a farmer and the dog that helps him. 'I have always liked animals,' says Bill, 'and dogs are so clever, they learn very quickly.'

Last year, the book was made into a film with real animals and actors. The film-makers used the latest computer technology to make people think that the animals are speaking. Bill was very pleased with the film. 'Sometimes film-makers change books, but they didn't change mine and I love the film.'

Paper 1 Reading and Writing

EXAMPLE	ANSWER
0 Bill Prince-Smith has had several jobs. **A** Right **B** Wrong **C** Doesn't say	**A**

21 Bill became a writer thirteen years ago.

   A Right   **B** Wrong   **C** Doesn't say

22 Bill writes his books in the evenings.

   A Right   **B** Wrong   **C** Doesn't say

23 Bill shows his writing to his wife.

   A Right   **B** Wrong   **C** Doesn't say

24 Bill writes books about his grandchildren.

   A Right   **B** Wrong   **C** Doesn't say

25 *The Sheepdog* was Bill's first book.

   A Right   **B** Wrong   **C** Doesn't say

26 Bill prefers writing about animals to writing about people.

   A Right   **B** Wrong   **C** Doesn't say

27 The film of *The Sheepdog* is different from the book.

   A Right   **B** Wrong   **C** Doesn't say

Test 2

PART 5

QUESTIONS 28–35

Read the article about an animal, the otter.
Choose the best word (A, B or C) for each space (28–35).
For questions 28–35, mark A, B or C on the answer sheet.

Otters

Not many people ......**0**...... seen an otter. These animals live ......**28**...... rivers and make their homes from small pieces of wood. They usually come ......**29**...... of their homes at night. Otters are very good in the water and can swim at more than 10 kilometres ......**30**...... hour. They have thick brown hair and this ......**31**...... them warm in the water. An otter can close ......**32**...... ears and nose. This means otters can stay under water ......**33**...... several minutes.

Twenty years ago, there were ......**34**...... otters in Great Britain. The water in the rivers was so dirty that many fish and insects died and the otters couldn't find anything to eat. But today there is lots of food for them ......**35**...... the rivers are clean again.

Paper 1 Reading and Writing

EXAMPLE							ANSWER
0	A	did	B	have	C	are	B

28	A	at	B	near	C	next
29	A	away	B	off	C	out
30	A	one	B	an	C	a
31	A	keeps	B	keep	C	kept
32	A	the	B	their	C	its
33	A	since	B	during	C	for
34	A	few	B	little	C	any
35	A	after	B	because	C	when

33

Test 2

PART 6

QUESTIONS 36–40

Read the descriptions (36–40) of some things you can see when you travel by road.
What is the word for each description?
The first letter is already there. There is one space for each other letter in the word.
For questions 36–40, write the words on the answer sheet.

EXAMPLE	ANSWER
0 You can drive fast here.	m o t o r w a y

36 Go here when you need petrol for your car. g _ _ _ _ _

37 This will take you over a river or another road. b _ _ _ _ _

38 You must show this person your driving licence if he asks for it. p _ _ _ _ _ _ _

39 You can go left, right or straight on at this place where two roads meet. c _ _ _ _ _ _ _

40 If these are red, the traffic has to wait. l _ _ _ _ _

PART 7

QUESTIONS 41–50

Complete these notes.
Write ONE word for each space (41–50).
For questions 41–50, write your words on the answer sheet.

TO ALL STUDENTS:

Would you (**Example:** ....*like*....) to come on a camping trip ....**41**.... weekend?

We are going to ....**42**.... to the forest in the school bus and we will stay at a camp-site ....**43**.... Friday to Sunday. ....**44**.... has hot showers and ....**45**.... small shop and you ....**46**.... rent bicycles there.

The trip ....**47**.... £25. It is very cold there ....**48**.... night, so you should take warm clothes and you will ....**49**.... to wear strong shoes.

....**50**.... you want to come, tell me today.

Ahmed
Student Secretary

Test 2

PART 8

QUESTIONS 51–55

Read the advertisement for summer jobs and the e-mail message.
Fill in the summer job application form.
For questions 51–55, write the information on the answer sheet.

**GRANTON UNIVERSITY
STUDENT JOBS
AUGUST**

Europe Computers:
   Cleaner, start next month.

Mill Farm:
   Fruit pickers, until end of this month

Brown's Hotel:
   Receptionist needed now, for 4 weeks, must speak a foreign language.

To: J & S Becker

Hi Mum and Dad!

My history course finishes on 28 July. I want to find a job for a month where I can practise my French and German and perhaps use a computer. I'll come back home to Canada in September.

Love
Helen

SUMMER JOB APPLICATION FORM

Name: *Helen Becker*

Nationality: **51** _____

University course: **52** _____

Foreign languages: **53** _____

Job wanted at: **54** _____

Which month can you work? **55** _____

PART 9

QUESTION 56

Read this note from your friend, Chris.

> Why didn't you come to the party last night?
>
> Can you meet me on Saturday? What do you want to do?
>
> Chris

Write a note to Chris. Answer the questions.

Write 25–35 words.

Write your note on the answer sheet.

Test 2

PAPER 2 LISTENING (approximately 30 minutes including 8 minutes transfer time)

PART 1

QUESTIONS 1–5

You will hear five short conversations.

You will hear each conversation twice.

There is one question for each conversation.

For questions 1–5, put a tick ✓ under the right answer.

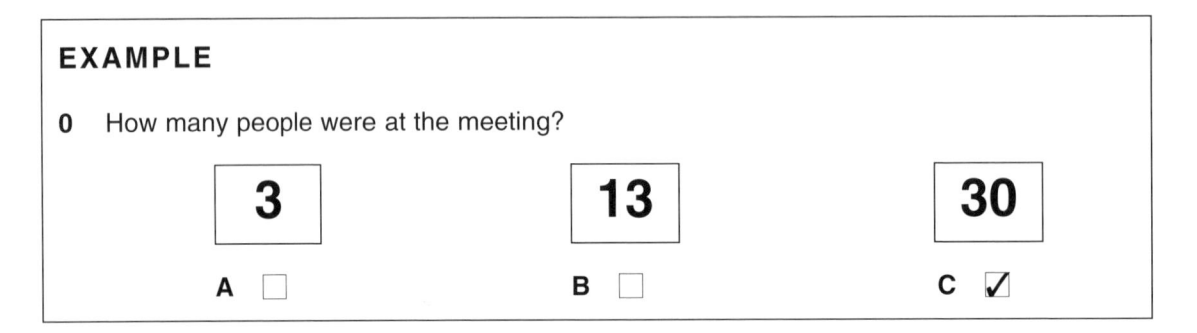

EXAMPLE

0   How many people were at the meeting?

3	13	30
A ☐	B ☐	C ✓

---

1   What colour is Kathy's bedroom now?

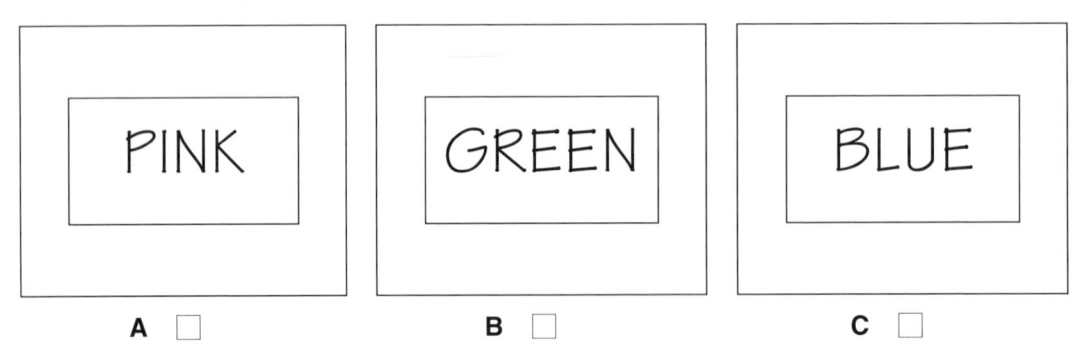

PINK	GREEN	BLUE
A ☐	B ☐	C ☐

2   Which platform does the woman's train leave from?

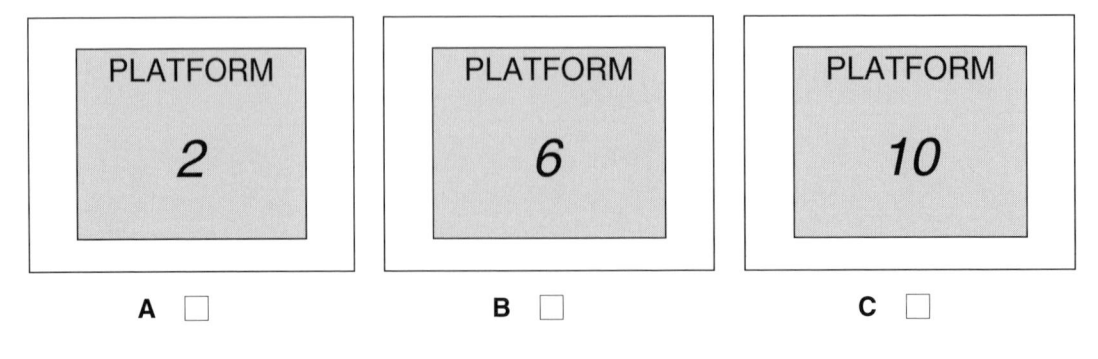

PLATFORM 2	PLATFORM 6	PLATFORM 10
A ☐	B ☐	C ☐

38

Paper 2 Listening

3 How is Susan going to get to the airport?

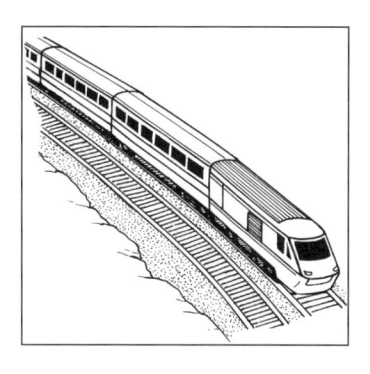

A ☐   B ☐   C ☐

4 Which is Anna's family?

A ☐   B ☐   C ☐

5 When is Kim's birthday party?

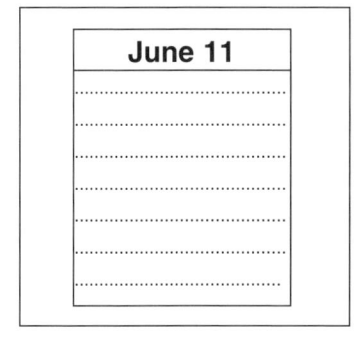

| June 11 | June 16 | June 30 |

A ☐   B ☐   C ☐

Test 2

PART 2

QUESTIONS 6–10

Listen to Rose talking to Steve about her day.
What is Rose going to do at each time?
For questions 6–10, write a letter A–H next to each time.
You will hear the conversation twice.

EXAMPLE

0   9.00 a.m.   E

TIMES

6   10.00 a.m.   ☐

7   11.00 a.m.   ☐

8   12.00 a.m.   ☐

9   1.00 p.m.   ☐

10 2.00 p.m.   ☐

ACTIVITIES

A   art lesson

B   have lunch

C   help Steve

D   meet Bill

E   see doctor

F   see teacher

G   study

H   swim

PART 3

QUESTIONS 11–15

Listen to Peter talking to a friend about learning to drive.

For questions 11–15, tick ✓ A, B or C.

You will hear the conversation twice.

EXAMPLE		ANSWER
0 The name of Peter's driving school is		
A AA.		☐
B AC.		☐
C ABC.		✓

11   Each driving lesson costs

   A   £14.   ☐

   B   £40.   ☐

   C   £60.   ☐

12   A lesson is

   A   30 minutes.   ☐

   B   45 minutes.   ☐

   C   60 minutes.   ☐

13   The teacher's car is

   A   slow.   ☐

   B   old.   ☐

   C   big.   ☐

Test 2

14 Peter failed the test because he

    A   drove too fast. ☐

    B   didn't see a crossing. ☐

    C   didn't stop at the traffic lights. ☐

15 Peter thinks the teacher is too

    A   expensive. ☐

    B   unfriendly. ☐

    C   young. ☐

PART 4

QUESTIONS 16–20

You will hear a man asking about theatre tickets.
Listen and complete questions 16–20.
You will hear the conversation twice.

PLAYHOUSE THEATRE

EVENING SHOW:		The White Room
Time:	16	
AFTERNOON SHOW:	17	The School
Time:		3 o'clock
Ticket prices:	18	£15 and £ ....
All tickets £6 on:	19	
Car park in:	20	.... Street

Test 2

PART 5

QUESTIONS 21–25

You will hear some information about a health centre.
Listen and complete questions 21–25.
You will hear the information twice.

MILL HOUSE HEALTH CENTRE

Opens again tomorrow at: 8 a.m.

Phone number (for appointments):   **21**

Phone after: **22**

Get medicines from: **23** .... Chemist's Shop

Bus number: **24**

For accidents, go to: **25** .... Hospital

You now have 8 minutes to write your answers on the answer sheet.

PAPER 3   SPEAKING (8–10 minutes)

The Speaking test lasts 8 to 10 minutes. You will take the test with another candidate. There are two examiners, but only one of them will talk to you. The examiner will ask you questions and ask you to talk to the other candidate.

Part 1 (5–6 minutes)

The examiner will ask you and your partner some questions. These questions will be about your daily life, past experience and future plans. For example, you may have to speak about your school, job, hobbies or home town.

Part 2 (3–4 minutes)

You and your partner will speak to each other. You will ask and answer questions. The examiner will give you a card with some information on it. The examiner will give your partner a card with some words on it. Your partner will use the words on the card to ask you questions about the information you have. Then you will change roles.

Test 3

PAPER 1 READING AND WRITING (1 hour 10 minutes)

PART 1
QUESTIONS 1–5

Which notice (A–H) says this (1–5)?
For questions 1–5, mark the correct letter A–H on the answer sheet.

EXAMPLE	ANSWER
0 We sell clothes.	F

1 This is only for young people.

2 Go to the next floor if you want a drink.

3 You cannot drive here today.

4 We are open every day.

5 Do not bring your lunch in here.

A MOTORWAY AHEAD – NO BICYCLES OR LEARNER DRIVERS

B COFFEE MACHINE UPSTAIRS

C DANGER – FOG! MOTORWAY CLOSED

D COMPUTER ROOM
No food or drinks inside

E Restaurant closed
Tuesday and Thursday lunchtime

F Ladies' and children's coats upstairs

G Kenyan Coffee Centre
Opening hours:
8 a.m. – 6 p.m. daily

H Under 12s swimming course
Saturday 10 a.m.

PART 2

QUESTIONS 6–10

Read the sentences (6–10) about a shopping trip.
Choose the best word (A, B or C) for each space.
For questions 6–10, mark A, B or C on the answer sheet.

EXAMPLE	ANSWER
0 Jack .... to buy a new pair of shoes for school.	C
A enjoyed B got C needed	

6 He .... a bus to the big department store in the centre of town.

    A travelled   B went   C took

7 The shoes were on the top .... near to the café.

    A stairs   B floor   C room

8 The assistant showed Jack several pairs but they were all the .... size.

    A wrong   B different   C big

9 Then he .... on some red and black leather football boots.

    A tried   B wore   C chose

10 'They're not too .... so I'll have them,' Jack said.

    A high   B great   C expensive

PART 3

QUESTIONS 11–15

Complete the five conversations.

For conversations 11–15, mark A, B or C on the answer sheet.

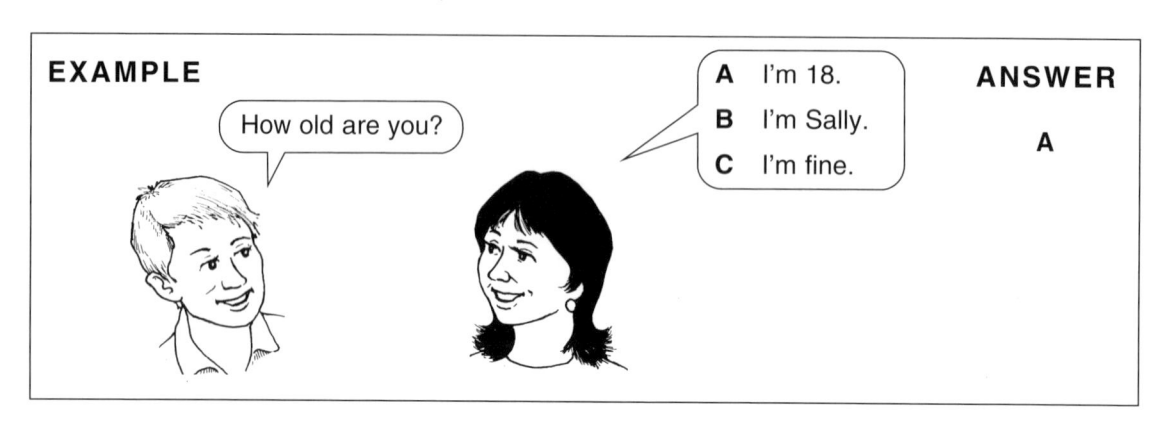

EXAMPLE

How old are you?

A I'm 18.
B I'm Sally.
C I'm fine.

ANSWER

A

11 It's my sister's birthday tomorrow!

A Happy New Year!
B Is she going to have a party?
C How old are they?

12 Mary will help the teacher.

A Are you certain?
B Do you understand?
C Can you hear?

13 I would like to see the doctor.

A I hope you'll feel better soon.
B It hurts a lot.
C Have you got an appointment?

14 Shall we leave now?

A Have you got time?
B Near the station?
C I'd like to stay.

15 Anything else?

A No, it isn't.
B Not at all.
C Not today, thanks.

Paper 1   Reading and Writing

QUESTIONS 16–20

Complete the conversation.
What does Chris say to the waiter?
For questions 16–20, mark the correct letter A–H on the answer sheet.

EXAMPLE		ANSWER
Waiter:	Good evening. Can I help you?	
Chris:	0	G

Waiter:	I'm afraid we haven't got a table free at the moment.	A	I'd like a salad and a main course.
Chris:	16	B	How long will we have to wait?
Waiter:	About a quarter of an hour. Those people in the corner have nearly finished.	C	Yes, we'll have two glasses of mineral water.
Chris:	17	D	Right. Where can we leave our coats?
Waiter:	Of course. Can I bring you a drink?	E	I need to make a telephone call.
Chris:	18	F	We'll go somewhere else.
Waiter:	Certainly. Anything else I can do for you?	G	Have you got a table for two, please?
Chris:	19	H	That's all right. Can we see the menu, please?
Waiter:	There's a phone outside the kitchen.		
Chris:	20		
Waiter:	I'll take them for you. Your table will be ready soon.		

PART 4

QUESTIONS 21–27

Read the article about some pop stars.

Are sentences 21–27 'Right' (A) or 'Wrong' (B)?

If there is not enough information to answer 'Right' (A) or 'Wrong' (B), choose 'Doesn't say' (C).

For questions 21–27, mark A, B or C on the answer sheet.

HOW DO THE IRISH POP-GROUP 'BOYZONE' LIVE A HEALTHY LIFE?

Stephen: Sleeping well is very important. When I can get home to my mother's house, I sleep for ten hours. But I find it very difficult to sleep at night after a concert because my head is full of music.

Keith: Sport is important. Before I had a car accident I was at the sports centre two and a half hours a day, five days a week. I can't do that now so I do about 150 sit-ups a day.

Ronan: I don't drink alcohol or smoke. I try to eat well. Also I drink a lot of water because it's good for your health. I should have about eight glasses a day but I don't always drink so much.

Shane: People shouldn't work all the time. I love my job but there are other things I like doing too. In my free time I just listen to music or watch TV. It's good for you to do nothing sometimes.

Mikey: I don't get tired any more since the doctor told me to eat better. Now I eat lots of things like carrots and spinach every day. But I still eat burgers sometimes!

Paper 1 Reading and Writing

EXAMPLE	ANSWER
0 Stephen sleeps well in his mother's house.	**A**
A Right **B** Wrong **C** Doesn't say	

21 Stephen thinks a lot about music after a concert.

   A Right   **B** Wrong   **C** Doesn't say

22 Keith's accident happened last year.

   A Right   **B** Wrong   **C** Doesn't say

23 Keith goes to the sports centre five days a week now.

   A Right   **B** Wrong   **C** Doesn't say

24 Ronan thinks he drinks enough water every day.

   A Right   **B** Wrong   **C** Doesn't say

25 Shane is only happy when he's working.

   A Right   **B** Wrong   **C** Doesn't say

26 Mikey was often tired before he started eating vegetables.

   A Right   **B** Wrong   **C** Doesn't say

27 Mikey's favourite food is burgers.

   A Right   **B** Wrong   **C** Doesn't say

PART 5

QUESTIONS 28–35

Read the article about a picture on a hill.
Choose the best word (A, B or C) for each space (28–35).
For questions 28–35, mark A, B or C on the answer sheet.

The Cerne Giant

Sherborne and Dorchester are two towns ......**0**...... the south of England that are quite near each other. On the road between them, ...**28**...... are a lot of green hills and fields. On one of ......**29**...... hills is a picture of a very large man. The man in the picture is called the *Cerne Giant* because the village that is ......**30**...... to him is called Cerne.

Nobody really ......**31**...... when the *Cerne Giant* was made, but people think that it was a very ......**32**...... time ago. To ......**33**...... nearer the picture, you can walk from Cerne. If you ......**34**...... on the first of May when the sun comes up, you will see all the people ......**35**...... the village dancing around the man on the hill.

Paper 1   Reading and Writing

EXAMPLE						ANSWER
0	A in	B on		C at		A

28	A there	B they	C where
29	A another	B its	C these
30	A beside	B next	C behind
31	A known	B knows	C know
32	A longest	B long	C longer
33	A get	B got	C getting
34	A go	B goes	C going
35	A on	B at	C from

Test 3

PART 6

QUESTIONS 36–40

Read the descriptions (36–40) of some things you may find at a party.
What is the word for each description?
The first letter is already there. There is one space for each other letter in the word.
For questions 36–40, write the words on the answer sheet.

EXAMPLE	ANSWER
0 Everybody likes to eat a piece of this.	c _a_ _k_ _e_

36   You need this if you want to dance.   m _ _ _ _

37   If it's your birthday, your guests may give you this.   p _ _ _ _ _ _

38   You need this to put your drink in.   g _ _ _ _

39   You can buy this drink in a bottle or a can.   l _ _ _ _ _ _

40   You hope these people will come to your party.   f _ _ _ _ _

PART 7

QUESTIONS 41–50

Complete the letter.
Write ONE word for each space (41–50).
For questions 41–50, write your words on the answer sheet.

Dear Lorna,

How (**Example:** *are*) you? I'm happy because **41** month I got a new job in the city centre. I **42** working in a Tourist Information Office and **43** is very interesting. I start work **44** morning at half past seven, so I **45** to get up very early! I love this job because I meet people from a **46** of different countries. I like telling them **47** our city. Here is **48** photo of me. I'm **49** my new uniform. **50** you like it?

Love,

Gloria

Test 3

PART 8

QUESTIONS 51–55

Read the two e-mail messages.

Fill in the Flower Order Form.

For questions 51–55, write the information on the answer sheet.

To:	Stephen Jones
Date:	21 August

Stephen!
Remember it's your sister's birthday tomorrow. She'll be 16. Have you got her new address in York? She lives in Shirley Road now, at number 47.

Mother

To:	Mary Jones
Date:	21 August

Don't worry Mum! I won't forget Lulu's special day tomorrow! I'm getting her some flowers – Garden Gate Flowers will send them for £15 or £20. I'll choose the cheaper ones, of course, with a nice card saying 'Happy Birthday'!

Stephen

Garden Gate Flowers
Flower Order Form

From: *Stephen Jones*

To: **51**

Date: **52**

Address: **53**

Price: **54**

Message on card: **55**

PART 9

QUESTION 56

You want to sell your bicycle and you see this notice at your college.

BICYCLE WANTED

HAVE YOU GOT A BICYCLE TO SELL?

HOW MUCH IS IT? HOW OLD IS IT?

WHEN CAN I SEE IT?

(Leave a note in reception for Gary Jones.)

Write a note to Gary Jones. Answer his questions about your bicycle.

Write 25–35 words.

Write your note on the answer sheet.

Test 3

PAPER 2   LISTENING (approximately 30 minutes including 8 minutes transfer time)

PART 1

QUESTIONS 1–5

You will hear five short conversations.

You will hear each conversation twice.

There is one question for each conversation.

For questions 1–5, put a tick ✓ under the right answer.

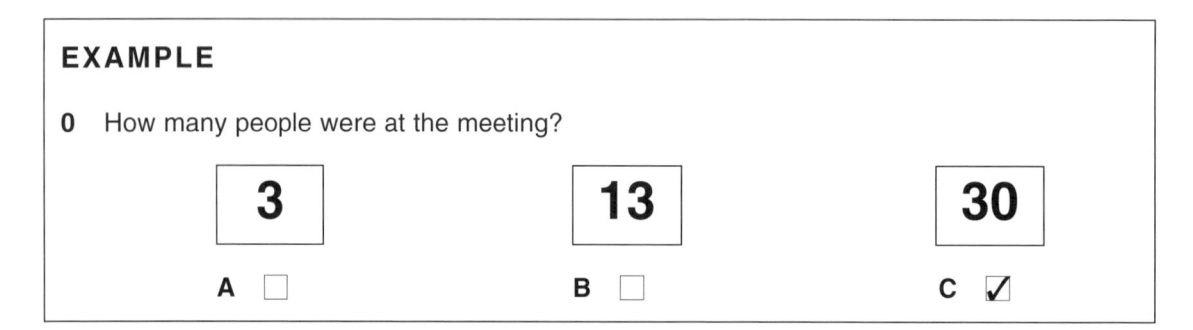

EXAMPLE

0 How many people were at the meeting?

3	13	30
A ☐	B ☐	C ✓

---

1 When will they go on holiday?

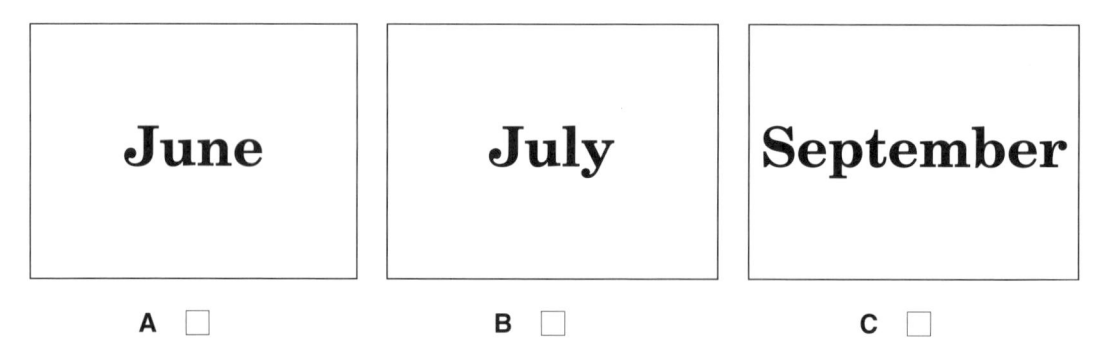

June	July	September
A ☐	B ☐	C ☐

2 How is Patti going to travel?

A ☐   B ☐   C ☐

58

Paper 2   Listening

3   What will Sam do?

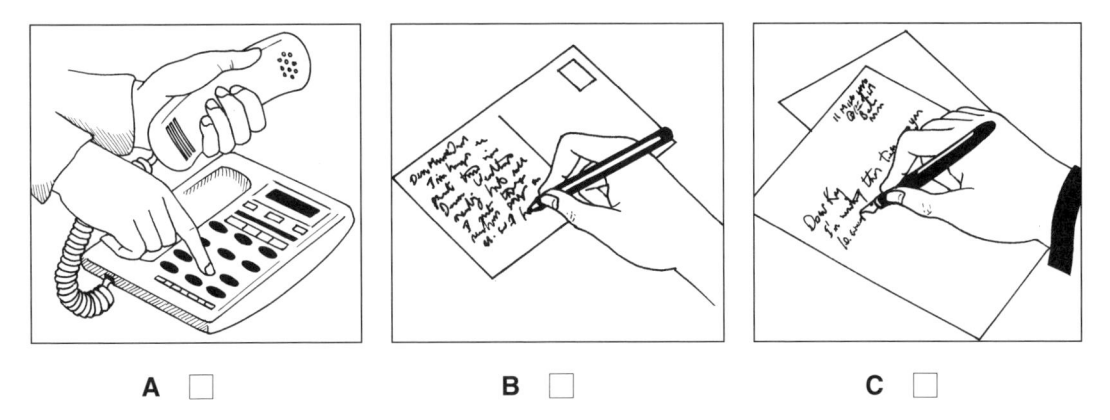

A ☐   B ☐   C ☐

4   What was the weather like in Portugal?

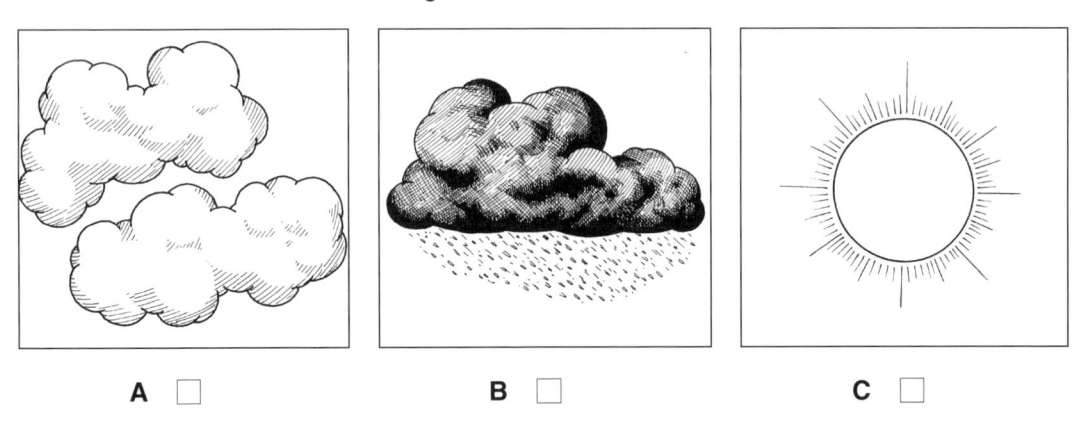

A ☐   B ☐   C ☐

5   What has the girl broken?

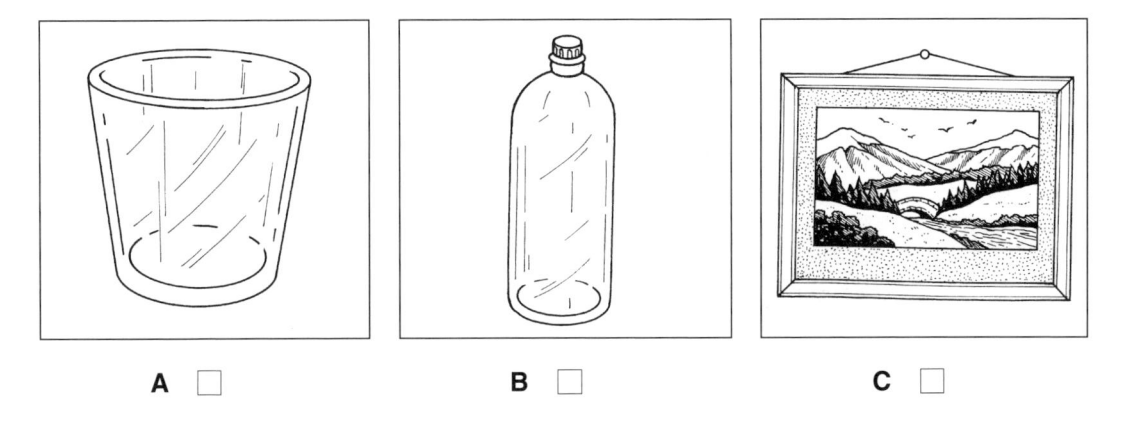

A ☐   B ☐   C ☐

Test 3

PART 2

QUESTIONS 6–10

Listen to Patrick talking to his mother about a photo of his old school friends.
What is each person wearing?
For questions 6–10, write a letter A–H next to each person.
You will hear the conversation twice.

EXAMPLE

0   Peter   D

PEOPLE

6   Martin

7   Joanna

8   Amy

9   James

10 Robert

THEIR CLOTHES

A   coat

B   dress

C   hat

D   jacket

E   jeans

F   shirt

G   sweater

H   t-shirt

Paper 2   Listening

PART 3

QUESTIONS 11–15

Listen to Jenny asking Mark about school holiday activities.
For questions 11–15, tick ☑ A, B or C.
You will hear the conversation twice.

EXAMPLE	ANSWER
0 The children's show is at	
A the theatre.	☐
B the shopping centre.	☐
C the library.	☑

11   The show begins at

    A   1.15. ☐

    B   2.00. ☐

    C   3.30. ☐

12   A child's ticket costs

    A   25p. ☐

    B   75p. ☐

    C   £1.50. ☐

13   The holiday reading course is for

    A   4 weeks. ☐

    B   6 weeks. ☐

    C   10 weeks. ☐

Test 3

14 This year from the library, children can win

    A a pen.

    B a school bag.

    C a book.

15 Jenny should meet Mark again

    A next week.

    B tomorrow.

    C today.

Paper 2   Listening

PART 4

QUESTIONS 16–20

You will hear Judy asking about music lessons.
Listen and complete questions 16–20.
You will hear the conversation twice.

GUITAR LESSONS FOR JUDY

Class: Beginners

Day: **16** _____

Starting time: **17** _____

Price of each lesson: **18** £ _____

Teacher's name: **19** Mrs _____

Room number: **20** _____

Test 3

PART 5

QUESTIONS 21–25

You will hear a teacher talking about a school trip.
Listen and complete questions 21–25.
You will hear the information twice.

SCHOOL TRIP

Day: Saturday

Visit: **21** _____

Leave at: **22** _____

Meet in: **23** _____

Cost: **24** £ _____

Bring: **25** _____

You now have 8 minutes to write your answers on the answer sheet.

PAPER 3 SPEAKING (8–10 minutes)

The Speaking test lasts 8 to 10 minutes. You will take the test with another candidate. There are two examiners, but only one of them will talk to you. The examiner will ask you questions and ask you to talk to the other candidate.

Part 1 (5–6 minutes)

The examiner will ask you and your partner some questions. These questions will be about your daily life, past experience and future plans. For example, you may have to speak about your school, job, hobbies or home town.

Part 2 (3–4 minutes)

You and your partner will speak to each other. You will ask and answer questions. The examiner will give you a card with some information on it. The examiner will give your partner a card with some words on it. Your partner will use the words on the card to ask you questions about the information you have. Then you will change roles.

Test 4

PAPER 1   READING AND WRITING (1 hour 10 minutes)

PART 1
QUESTIONS 1–5

Which notice (A–H) says this (1–5)?
For questions 1–5, mark the correct letter A–H on the answer sheet.

EXAMPLE	ANSWER
0 You can only get small pictures here.	H

1 You can use this for two days.

2 Students do not have to pay to go here at weekends.

3 Someone would like to speak another language.

4 If you study here, you will pay less for this.

5 You can find things to listen to here in the college.

A
WANTED
Spanish lessons
evenings or weekends

B
English Language Student Library
books, magazines and cassettes

C
College Film Night
'TITANIC'
College students £2.50   Others £3.00

D
The Biggest Video Store in Town
OPEN 24 HOURS

E
YORK MUSEUM
Mon–Fri   £5
Sat–Sun   £2 / Students free

F
**Weekend Travel Card £10
Train or Bus
Central London only**

G
Learn to play the guitar in four months
Video course – £50

H
Colour Photos
Passport size only 4 for £3

PART 2

QUESTIONS 6–10

Read the sentences (6–10) about Jane's hobby.
Choose the best word (A, B or C) for each space.
For questions 6–10, mark A, B or C on the answer sheet.

EXAMPLE			ANSWER
0 Jane's .... hobby is taking photographs.			B
A happy	B favourite	C excellent	

6   She hopes to .... a photographer for a newspaper one day.

    A   work   B   become   C   do

7   She .... a photography club to learn more about using a camera.

    A   made   B   went   C   joined

8   Jane says it's .... to take pictures of children or animals because they are always moving.

    A   careful   B   hard   C   fast

9   There was a .... about a competition in a photography magazine.

    A   notice   B   bill   C   ticket

10   Jane .... the first prize for one of her pictures.

    A   won   B   carried   C   caught

Test 4

PART 3

QUESTIONS 11–15

Complete the five conversations.

For conversations 11–15, mark A, B or C on the answer sheet.

EXAMPLE

Where do you come from?

A New York.
B School.
C Home.

ANSWER

A

---

11 When will lunch be ready?

A Quite soon.
B It's soup and toast.
C I hope you're hungry.

12 It's very hot in here.

A Do you feel cold?
B I'll turn on the heating.
C Let's go outside then.

13 Have you met Henry before?

A Yes, at first.
B Yes, on holiday.
C Yes, I do.

14 Do you like visiting museums?

A I'd love to!
B No, I haven't.
C Not really.

15 I've broken my glasses.

A Here's another one.
B You can't see.
C That's a pity!

QUESTIONS 16–20

Complete the conversation.
What does the student say to the assistant in the tourist information office?
For questions 16–20, mark the correct letter A–H on the answer sheet.

EXAMPLE	ANSWER
Assistant: Hello, can I help you?	
Student: 0	H

PART 4

QUESTIONS 21–27

Read the article about a singer.

Are sentences 21–27 'Right' (A) or 'Wrong' (B)?

If there is not enough information to answer 'Right' (A) or 'Wrong' (B), choose 'Doesn't say' (C).

For questions 21–27, mark A, B or C on the answer sheet.

John Pickering

In a park in a small town in central England, John Pickering cuts the grass and waters the flowers. But all last week he was in Tokyo and millions of Japanese people watched the thirty-five-year-old gardener on television because John is the number one singer in Japan at the moment. John visited Japan a few months ago to sing in dance clubs in Osaka and Nagoya. A disc jockey heard his songs and played them on his radio show. Hundreds of young people phoned the radio and asked the disc jockey to play the songs once more.

John, who uses the name Jon Otis when he sings in Japan, is not going to stop working in the park in England. He does not know yet how much he will earn from his music. 'I must keep my job in the park,' he says. 'I still have to pay my bills!' The other gardeners do not know that he is famous in Japan. They've never even heard him sing.

John's wife, Denise, a hospital worker, says, 'This will not change the way we live. I only know John Pickering, not Jon Otis!'

Paper 1   Reading and Writing

EXAMPLE	ANSWER
0 John Pickering usually works in England.	**A**
A Right **B** Wrong **C** Doesn't say	

21   A few days ago, John was on television in Japan.

A Right   **B** Wrong   **C** Doesn't say

22   John's first show in Japan was on the radio.

A Right   **B** Wrong   **C** Doesn't say

23   John hopes to become famous in England one day.

A Right   **B** Wrong   **C** Doesn't say

24   John Pickering and Jon Otis are the same person.

A Right   **B** Wrong   **C** Doesn't say

25   John will still work in the park because he needs the money.

A Right   **B** Wrong   **C** Doesn't say

26   John's colleagues think his songs are very good.

A Right   **B** Wrong   **C** Doesn't say

27   John's wife would like him to stop singing.

A Right   **B** Wrong   **C** Doesn't say

Test 4

PART 5

QUESTIONS 28–35

Read the article about postcards.
Choose the best word (A, B or C) for each space (28–35).
For questions 28–35, mark A, B or C on the answer sheet.

POSTCARDS

Today, people like to send postcards ......**0**...... their friends and family. These postcards often ......**28**...... pictures of beaches, mountains or castles on them and you ......**29**...... write a message on the back. Many people send postcards ......**30**...... they are on holiday because postcards are cheap and the pictures on them are often ......**31**...... than people's own photos.

Somebody sent the first postcard ......**32**...... the end of the nineteenth century. It had a picture of a town by the sea on it. Later on, postcards had pictures showing something in the news that week, perhaps an accident ......**33**...... an important person's visit. People liked to ......**34**...... them because they did ......**35**...... have pictures in their newspapers then.

72

Paper 1 Reading and Writing

EXAMPLE						ANSWER
0	A to	B	by	C	from	A

28	A	had	B	has	C	have
29	A	can	B	shall	C	do
30	A	until	B	when	C	during
31	A	best	B	better	C	good
32	A	at	B	in	C	on
33	A	also	B	too	C	or
34	A	see	B	saw	C	seen
35	A	never	B	not	C	no

73

PART 6

QUESTIONS 36–40

Read the descriptions (36–40) of some things you may learn about in a geography lesson.

What is the word for each description?

The first letter is already there. There is one space for each other letter in the word.

For questions 36–40, write the words on the answer sheet.

EXAMPLE	ANSWER
0 This is a large group of trees.	f _o_ _r_ _e_ _s_ _t_

36 You may find snow on the top of this at all times of the year.   m _ _ _ _ _ _ _

37 The farmer puts animals or plants here.   f _ _ _ _ _

38 People have to cross water to get to this.   i _ _ _ _ _ _

39 The water in this starts in the hills and runs to the sea.   r _ _ _ _

40 Engineers build this to take things in boats from one place to another.   c _ _ _ _

PART 7

QUESTIONS 41–50

Complete the letter.
Write ONE word for each space (41–50).
For questions 41–50, write your words on the answer sheet.

Dear Mrs Brian,

I (**Example:** ....*am*....) sorry but I can't come to your class ....**41**.... more because I have ....**42**.... return to my country. My sister is going to get married ....**43**.... month. I want to go shopping ....**44**.... her to choose a dress. My parents ....**45**.... going to make a big meal for the guests and there will ....**46**.... a lot of work in the kitchen.

I'm sorry I ....**47**.... leave the English class. You are ....**48**.... very good teacher. Please ....**49**.... goodbye to the other students for ....**50**.... .

Thanks again.

Best wishes,

Soraya

PART 8

QUESTIONS 51–55

Read the note and the information about music lessons.

Fill in the information on the application form.

For questions 51–55, write the information on the answer sheet.

Dear Mrs Bell,

I would like to join your piano class. I can play some classical music, but now I'd like to learn to play modern music. I have English classes with Mr Smith every morning, but I am free in the afternoons.

Maria Gomez

MUSIC LESSONS

Mrs Bell

Wednesday	10 am	Piano
	2 pm	Guitar
Thursday	9.30 am	Guitar
	3.30 pm	Piano

College Music Lessons Application Form

Name:	*Maria Gomez*
Teacher:	51
Musical instrument:	52
What kind of music do you want to learn?	53
Day of class:	54
Time of class:	55

PART 9

QUESTION 56

You are going to go walking with your English friend next Friday. Write a note to your friend.

Say:

- **where** you can go walking
- **what** you are going to wear
- **what** your friend should bring.

Write 25–35 words.

Write your note on the answer sheet.

Test 4

PAPER 2 LISTENING (approximately 30 minutes including 8 minutes transfer time)

PART 1

QUESTIONS 1–5

You will hear five short conversations.

You will hear each conversation twice.

There is one question for each conversation.

For questions 1–5, put a tick ✓ under the right answer.

EXAMPLE

0   How many people were at the meeting?

3	13	30
A ☐	B ☐	C ✓

---

1   Which is Tom's mother?

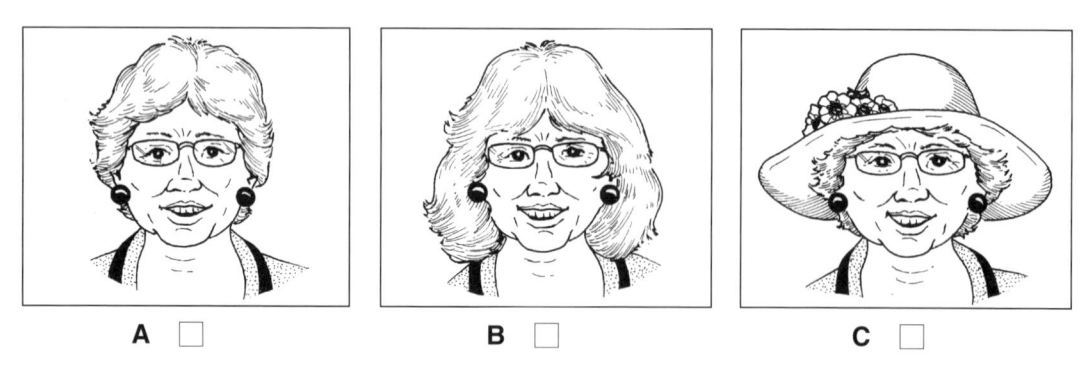

A ☐   B ☐   C ☐

2   Where will the beach party be?

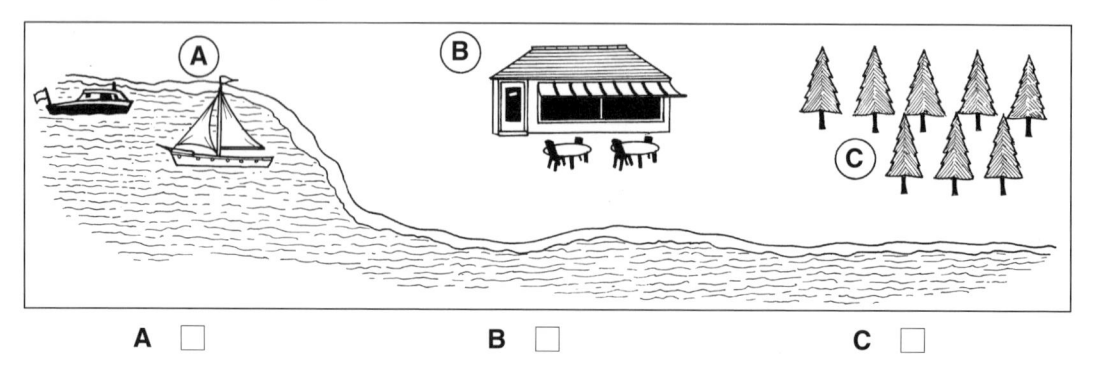

A ☐   B ☐   C ☐

78

Paper 2   Listening

3   What will Fiona wear to the dance?

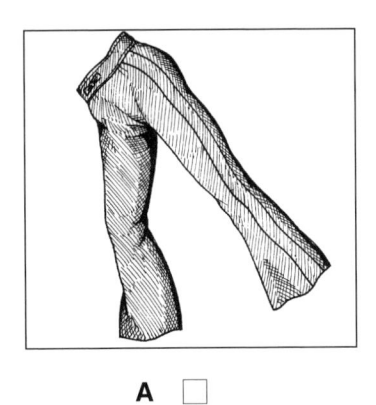

A 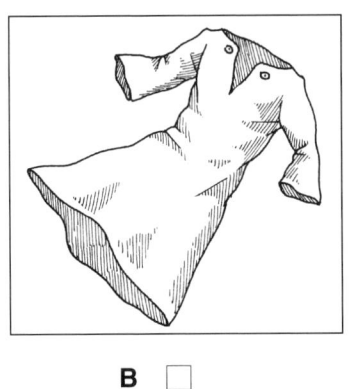 ☐   B 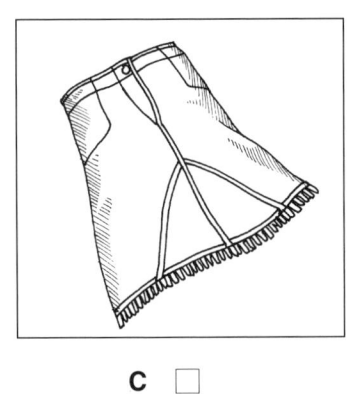 ☐   C ☐

4   What homework is the girl doing now?

Science   **Maths**   **English**

A ☐   B ☐   C ☐

5   What's David going to buy?

A 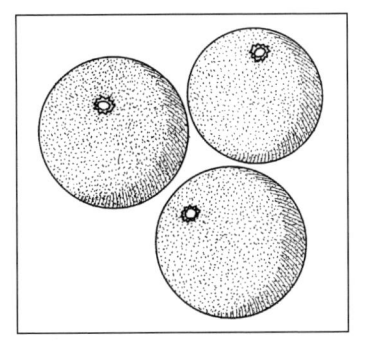 ☐   B  ☐   C ☐

79

Test 4

PART 2

QUESTIONS 6–10

Listen to Sonya talking to Martin about her family.
How old are her brothers and sisters?
For questions 6–10, write a letter A–H next to each person.
You will hear the conversation twice.

EXAMPLE

0   Sonya   H

PEOPLE   **AGES**

6   Sally   ☐   A   two

7   Vivienne   ☐   B   five

                                C   seven

8   Roger   ☐
                                D   ten

9   Frank   ☐   E   thirteen

                                F   fifteen
10 Deborah   ☐

                                G   eighteen

                                H   twenty

PART 3

QUESTIONS 11–15

Listen to a woman asking a travel agent for some information about a park in the mountains.

For questions 11–15, tick ✓ A, B or C.

You will hear the conversation twice.

EXAMPLE	ANSWER
0 The woman will visit the park for	
A one week.	✓
B two weeks.	☐
C four weeks.	☐

11 In the park, there is

    A a café. ☐

    B a hotel. ☐

    C a guest-house. ☐

12 The village has a

    A swimming pool. ☐

    B cinema. ☐

    C food shop. ☐

13 You can only go through the park

    A by car. ☐

    B by bus. ☐

    C on foot. ☐

Test 4

14 On weekdays, a visit to the park costs

    A $12.   ☐

    B $13.   ☐

    C $16.   ☐

15 In the park, the woman will see

    A   animals.   ☐

    B   flowers.   ☐

    C   snow.   ☐

Paper 2   Listening

PART 4

QUESTIONS 16–20

You will hear Mats talking to his friend, Sarah, about a trip to Manchester in England.
Listen and complete questions 16–20.
You will hear the conversation twice.

TRIP TO MANCHESTER

Go to Manchester in:	October
Temperature in autumn:	**16** .... degrees
Will need to wear:	**17**
Name of train station in London:	**18**
Cost of train:	**19** £
Take Sarah some:	**20**

Test 4

PART 5

QUESTIONS 21–25

You will hear some information about a museum.

Listen and complete questions 21–25.

You will hear the information twice.

THE REDFERN MUSEUM

Open: Monday to Thursday

You can see:

Downstairs **21** old ....

Upstairs: pictures by **22** .... artists

Concerts during month of: **23**

Student ticket: **24** £

Telephone number: **25**

You now have 8 minutes to write your answers on the answer sheet.

PAPER 3 SPEAKING (8–10 minutes)

The Speaking test lasts 8 to 10 minutes. You will take the test with another candidate. There are two examiners, but only one of them will talk to you. The examiner will ask you questions and ask you to talk to the other candidate.

Part 1 (5–6 minutes)

The examiner will ask you and your partner some questions. These questions will be about your daily life, past experience and future plans. For example, you may have to speak about your school, job, hobbies or home town.

Part 2 (3–4 minutes)

You and your partner will speak to each other. You will ask and answer questions. The examiner will give you a card with some information on it. The examiner will give your partner a card with some words on it. Your partner will use the words on the card to ask you questions about the information you have. Then you will change roles.

Visual materials for Paper 3

1A

The White House
Disco

Rock music from the U.S.A.

Over 18s only

Doors open: 9 pm
Tuesday – Saturday

Tickets: £6 (Students £5)
No jeans or T-shirts

2B

ART SHOW

- where?

- when?

- whose pictures?

- ticket? £

- buy / picture?

Visual materials

3A

Parker's Sweet Shop

14 Barrett Road
5 minutes from town centre

TRY OUR FAMOUS CHOCOLATE EGGS AND SUGAR HEARTS

Prices lower than in other shops

OPEN MONDAY–SATURDAY 9AM–5PM

4B

A WALK FOR TOURISTS

- where / start?

- what / visit?

- every day?

- expensive?

- lunch?

Visual materials

1B

DISCO

- every evening?

- what music?

- clothes / wear?

- student ticket? £?

- begin?

2A

ART SHOW

Pictures by David Piper

Meet the artist and buy a painting for your home

6–8pm every evening

Adults: £4
Students: £2

28 Market Street

3B

SWEET SHOP

- **name?**

- **expensive?**

- **when / open?**

- **chocolate eggs?**

- **near town centre?**

4A

WALK THROUGH OUR BEAUTIFUL TOWN
FRIENDLY TOUR GUIDES

See the museum, market and castle

Every Tuesday
Starts: Grand Hotel at 10 am
Finishes with lunch in Park Restaurant

£13 per person

Visual materials

1C

PAINTING COMPETITION

For young people 8–16 years old

Paint a picture of an animal

Send it to:
Young Artist Magazine
12 High Street

before 14 September

and win a bicycle!

2D

FILM CLUB

- **every week?**

- **price? £**

- **where / ticket?**

- **French films?**

- **café?**

3C

GLORIA'S SANDWICH SHOP

We make 100 different sandwiches!

Hot soup
Orange juice
Coffee

£2.80 each sandwich

Car park behind shop

Closed on Mondays

4D

CLUB FOR YOUNG PEOPLE

- name?

- when?

- what / do?

- where?

- cost? £?

Visual materials

1D

PAINTING COMPETITION

- ◆ win something?

- ◆ what / paint?

- ◆ for everybody?

- ◆ competition address?

- ◆ last day?

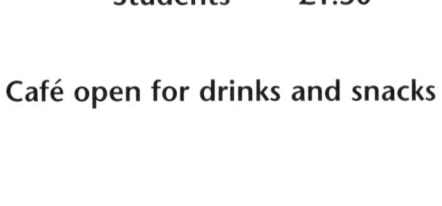

2C

CITY UNIVERSITY FILM CLUB

EVERY MONDAY 6–9.30 p.m.

Films from America, Australia and Britain

Get your tickets from the Student Office

| Adults | £3 |
| Students | £1.50 |

Café open for drinks and snacks

3D

SANDWICH SHOP

- what sandwiches?

- price?

- open every day?

- drinks?

- car park?

4C

HAPPY DAYS CLUB

for young people from
12–18 years

Every Friday
7.30–10.30 pm

29 Milton Street

Just £2 per week

Games – music – dancing and lots more

Sample answer sheet – Reading and Writing (Sheet 1)

UNIVERSITY of CAMBRIDGE
ESOL Examinations

SAMPLE

Candidate Name
If not already printed, write name in CAPITALS and complete the Candidate No. grid (in pencil).

Candidate Signature

Examination Title

Centre

Supervisor:
If the candidate is ABSENT or has WITHDRAWN shade here

Centre No.

Candidate No.

Examination Details

KET Paper 1 Reading and Writing Candidate Answer Sheet

Instructions

Use a PENCIL (B or HB).
Rub out any answer you want to change with an eraser.

For **Parts 1, 2, 3, 4** and **5**:
Mark ONE letter for each question.
For example, if you think **C** is the right answer to the question, mark your answer sheet like this:

| 0 | A B C |

Part 1
1 A B C D E F G H
2 A B C D E F G H
3 A B C D E F G H
4 A B C D E F G H
5 A B C D E F G H

Part 2
6 A B C
7 A B C
8 A B C
9 A B C
10 A B C

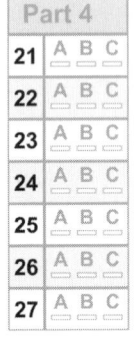

Part 3
11 A B C
12 A B C
13 A B C
14 A B C
15 A B C

16 A B C D E F G H
17 A B C D E F G H
18 A B C D E F G H
19 A B C D E F G H
20 A B C D E F G H

Part 4
21 A B C
22 A B C
23 A B C
24 A B C
25 A B C
26 A B C
27 A B C

Part 5
28 A B C
29 A B C
30 A B C
31 A B C
32 A B C
33 A B C
34 A B C
35 A B C

Turn over for Parts 6 - 9 →

© UCLES K&J Photocopiable

Sample answer sheet – Reading and Writing (Sheet 2)

For **Parts 6, 7 and 8**:
Write your answers in the spaces next to the numbers (36 to 55) like this:

| 0 | example |

Part 6		Do not write here
36		1 36 0
37		1 37 0
38		1 38 0
39		1 39 0
40		1 40 0

Part 7		Do not write here
41		1 41 0
42		1 42 0
43		1 43 0
44		1 44 0
45		1 45 0
46		1 46 0
47		1 47 0
48		1 48 0
49		1 49 0
50		1 50 0

Part 8		Do not write here
51		1 51 0
52		1 52 0
53		1 53 0
54		1 54 0
55		1 55 0

Part 9 (Question 56): Write your answer below.

Do not write below (Examiner use only)

0 1 2 3 4 5

© UCLES K&J Photocopiable

Sample answer sheet – Listening

UNIVERSITY of CAMBRIDGE
ESOL Examinations

SAMPLE

Candidate Name
If not already printed, write name in CAPITALS and complete the Candidate No. grid (in pencil).

Candidate Signature

Examination Title

Centre

Supervisor:
If the candidate is ABSENT or has WITHDRAWN shade here

Centre No.

Candidate No.

Examination Details

KET Paper 2 Listening Candidate Answer Sheet

Instructions

Use a PENCIL (B or HB).

Rub out any answer you want to change with an eraser.

For **Parts 1, 2** and **3**:
Mark ONE letter for each question.
For example, if you think **C** is the right answer to the question, mark your answer sheet like this:

0 | A B C

Part 1	Part 2	Part 3
1 A B C	6 A B C D E F G H	11 A B C
2 A B C	7 A B C D E F G H	12 A B C
3 A B C	8 A B C D E F G H	13 A B C
4 A B C	9 A B C D E F G H	14 A B C
5 A B C	10 A B C D E F G H	15 A B C

For **Parts 4** and **5**:
Write your answers in the spaces next to the numbers (16 to 25) like this:

0 | example

Part 4		Do not write here	Part 5		Do not write here
16		1 16 0	21		1 21 0
17		1 17 0	22		1 22 0
18		1 18 0	23		1 23 0
19		1 19 0	24		1 24 0
20		1 20 0	25		1 25 0

© UCLES K&J Photocopiable